Milo Defonz Codding

The Issues of the Hour

Political and Military

Milo Defonz Codding

The Issues of the Hour
Political and Military

ISBN/EAN: 9783337133917

Printed in Europe, USA, Canada, Australia, Japan

Cover: Foto ©ninafisch / pixelio.de

More available books at **www.hansebooks.com**

ISSUES OF THE HOUR,

POLITICAL AND MILITARY:

BEING

REMINISCENCES AND CONCLUSIONS.

THE CONGEALED ANGUISH OF THE OPPRESSED, ERST
THE TAPESTRY OF HEAVEN, DISSOLVED BY THE
TEARS OF THE BEREAVED, RETURNING,
COMES TO BE THE SYMBOLS OF A
PEOPLE'S DESOLATION.

ROCHESTER, N. Y.:
MILO DEFONZ, AUTHOR AND PUBLISHER.
1863.

THE ISSUES OF THE HOUR.

*" I feel that Republicanism is extinct in our country. We are
ruled by an Oligarchy, and they are waiting only a convenient
opportunity for setting aside the forms of Republicanism."*

Such were the words, *verbatim*, of a slaveholding planter of
Georgia—by name Davis—spoken to the writer on board the
steamer from Wilmington, North Carolina, to Charleston, South
Carolina, during the beautiful afternoon of the fourth of July,
A. D., 1850.

In view of the circumstance that it was the concluding element of the most exciting day the writer had then experienced,
a vivid recollection of the remark will not appear surprising,
and its having proved itself the key to the greatest problem
any people were ever required to solve, is sufficient occasion
for making it the opening text of this discussion.

Mr. Davis had proved himself a sincere friend, a patriotic
gentlemen, and a conscientious slavocrat. He, with two others,
all entire strangers to the writer, had quelled the rising of a
mob, upon the cars, which had threatened to lynch this North-
erner, because, that while riding through the turpentine forest
of North Carolina, before breakfast, on the morning of the
Fourth of July, he had conversed with his seat-mate, a Caro-
linian, upon the principles of the Declaration of Independence.
The conversation had been introduced by the query: " Why
don't you abolish slavery down here—your country looks as

though the genius of desolation had brooded over it for centuries." My seat-mate had just entered the cars, and as he sat down, remarked: "It is eighteen miles to breakfast." Not a word of a specially irritating or exciting character had been spoken, but on leaving the car there was a continual fire in the rear, of such expressions as "He ought to be lynched;" "Its good enough for him;" "D—n him," etc.

On reaching the door of the car, the object of the threats turned and replied: "You are a brave set, priding yourselves upon your chivalrous gallantry, and talk of lynching an unarmed stranger in your midst, for talking about the Declaration of Independence on the Fourth of July.

A Creole, of New Orleans—name not given—gently tapped the speaker on the shoulder from behind, and earnestly, but emphatically, whispered, "*Hist! Hist!*" And as the writer's eyes again sought the hotel, charged him, at his peril, to keep quiet. That gentleman comprehended the game, and remained to soothe the irate "Chivalry." All now seemed quiet, but while waiting upon the piazza for a chance at the wash-basin. one Captain McGowan, from the Mexican war, a cotton manufacturer by slave labor, of Georgia, and son of a former Governor of that State, taking a knife from his pocket, opened it, and with his hand wiping the blade, which was about seven inches in length, shook it at the stranger, exclaiming: "That is a Southern argument, G—d d—n you—I told you not to say anything on that subject farther South!" This referred to a long conversation of the previous day, at Petersburg, Virginia. where we had been detained twenty-four hours, by the stoppage of the train, a log being placed upon the track by a negro whom the Conductor had previously abused. The Captain had in this conversation made one important admission. that "In consequence of the truthful representation the Abolitionists had made of the scanty fare of slaves, the masters had increased their food and raiment to just double what it had previously been." But to the gallant Southerner's present threatening exhibition, the response was a quiet folding of the arms and

the remark : " We Northerners carry our arguments in our
hats." Too unsuspecting to dream of being in the least
danger, this ninny had unconsciously played the hero. The
gallant Captain lost color, closed his knife, and while returning
it to his pocket, exclaimed : "You are the d—est courageous
man I ever met." Upon reflection it came to appear that the
position had been the proper one for defense, in case of attack ;
and the Captain had doubtless imagined the presence of con-
cealed weapons.

Breakfast over, a seat in the car was resumed, the Creole
friend took the seat back of it, Mr. Davis the one opposite him,
a lady—young, but with a gritty upper lip—sat opposite
the stranger, and a young professional gentleman the next forward of the lady.

One of them immediately opened with the remark : "Now
we want to discuss slavery with you." I declined, saying : "I
have tested the Southern character, and found you are not the
generous and hospitable people you are set up to be." They
were not to be put off, and the subject was discussed till our
arrival at Wilmington, at noon. Mr. Davis closing his part of
the argument by saying : " If you will spend ten days with me,
I will give you a plantation, slaves and all, if you do not at that
time admit that it has changed your views of the subject." To
this I replied : " My conviction is, that it would only increase my
aversion to the institution, as all that I have seen of it has
done ; that it did not seem just for me to accept his liberal offer,
though I should like to visit his place." Next morning the
friends came to me, as we were in sight of Charleston, and with
every exhibition of friendly interest, besought me as my life
was valued, not to give utterance there to the least syllable of
disapprobation of slavery. But as we were passing Fort
Sumter, now so famous, the Captain (McGowan), pointing to
its warlike aspect, remarked : "See what you will have to meet
when there comes a war between the North and the South."

To the words of our text, we had replied : "It may appear
so from your stand-point, but be assured that when this oligarchy

comes to make the attempt to set aside the forms of Republicanism, it will awake at the North an under-current of which they little dream." He replied: "What is it—is it the Abolition Party?" "No." "What then?" "It is the inherent feeling with which every child grows up; that he sucks in with his mother's milk; that he is a part of the Government of these United States." "So long as they are privileged to drop the ballot for choice of the servants who for them administer the Government, they may remain quiet, although crafty men control the result. But once take from them the forms of self-government, the North will arise in unity and power as one man, for the preservation of their liberties."

Why was it that thirteen years since, passengers in a railroad car, traversing the gloomy turpentine forests of North Carolina, should become frenzied at the mention of the fundamental principles of the Declaration of American Independence?

Why would have ensued a similar excitement, with most likely a fiendish execution of diabolical threats, had the scene been laid, not even in any populous district of slavedom, but among the forsaken everglades of Florida, or amid the desolations of the most tenantless portions of the Alleghanies?

Why was it, that during the thirty years preceding the rebellion, those who have been constant in their clamor about the guaranties of the Constitution, have as constantly illustrated their hollow-heartedness by such a disregard of its most important provisions, as to annihilate "the freedom of speech," "the rights of citizenship," and "the rights of States," while travelling through, or sojourning in, any part of the slave country?

Why was it, that while the South were dependent upon the North for their teachers, and much other service, it was only by a lie on the lips, and with life in the hands, that an American citizen could do business in its midst, or even travel there?

Aye, all this and much else, is answered by those portentous words : " We are ruled by an Oligarchy, and they are waiting only a convenient opportunity for setting aside the forms of Republicanism."

Ruled by an Oligarchy! American citizens ruled by an Oligarchy ! O shade of the immortal founders of the American Republic ! The country you freed from the political despotism of the Old World, in the life of one generation, come to be ruled by an Oligarchy, before the weight of whose despotism that of Britain becomes lost in lightness !

Here, then, we have the essential *fact*, that this rebellion was all arranged, and settled, and provided for, more than ten years before its final culmination to a practical issue. Hence it is easy to comprehend what was meant by the assertions of the members of this same " Oligarchy," when asserting that they would yet call the muster-roll of their slaves upon immortal Bunker Hill, and in the sacred shade of its monument. All this formerly passed as idle gasconade, but does so no longer.

But whence came this Oligarchy? What were its originating causes? What the antecedents of its constituents and abettors? What their aims—and what their hopes of accomplishment? All this is necessary to be understood by the republican elements of American society—and which includes all who to-day desire the perpetuity of free republican institutions. And it will not be out of place to, also, in such connection, exhibit the origin of the republican ideas, the republican people, and the republican powers, of America. That republicanism to which we owe all that is superior in the appertainments of American life. And for this discussion it is necessary to revert briefly to the original settlement of this continent by the English, and to the then existing classes of British society.

The first English settlement in America was in Virginia, and developed as a purely speculative adventure. Neither morals, religion, nor politics, had the least possible influence in the enterprise—and perhaps it would not do the original settlers any degree of injustice to add, that many of them were actuated by wholesome desire to escape the restraints of the first, the annoyances of the second, or the inflctions of the judicial department of the last. Certainly there existed in Britain at that time two essentially different classes of people—made such, by difference in the fundamental principles of their religious systems—or rather, by adopting religious formulas corresponding to their own innate characters. The great majority of the British people developed a religion of a quality which did not effectually interfere with the Cainish principle, that might makes right, and that any advantage of the strong over the weak is right, so long as the practical powers of judicial processes cannot be successfully applied to prevent spoliation. Such was also the quality of the religious ethics of the Waldenses, who settled in South Carolina—the Spanish, in Florida—the French, in Louisiana—and the English Papists, who settled Maryland.

The other religious system of Britain, and which includes all sects of Dissenters from the political churches, was based upon the principle that, Right, and Wrong, were absolute qualities, not in the least varied by the incidental advantages, or disadvantages, of either party. That the starting point of religious rectitude, and moral character, was a determination to do justice to all, as the highest duty of life, and a paramount obligation to God, and to man.

The intense purity of life, exacted by the religious formulas of the votaries of this type of ethics, evoked for them the cognomen of Puritans, a title destined to become the most honored of all which history of the past will transmit to future times. Persecuted from home by the religion of the state, the Puritans settled in New England, where the asperity of the climate forbid most speculations, except the cultivation of schoolhouses, meetinghouses and printinghouses. New York had already been settled by the Dutch of similar principles, and the Friends in Pennsylvania, and the Presbyterians in New Jersey, filled up the map of the original provinces of that country, whose descendants will forever glory in having been the original settlers of Puritania.

An exceedingly curious, as well as intensely interesting circumstance, illustrative of the opposite characteristics of the settlers of the two regions now at deadly strife of both arms, and ideas, was the fact, that while the first ship load of Puritans were crossing the Atlantic in search of a speck of God's earth upon which they might be privileged to practise right between man and man, and perpetuate that virtue by a conscientious worship of God—another vessel was also crossing the same ocean, with the first cargo of emigrants from a different continent, another race of men—not voluntary travellers—but stolen captives, the victims of the stronger—captured, enslaved and transported to a distant wilderness of a different climate— and doomed with their posterity, to an existence of the most abject, and rewardless servitude.

That total disregard of the ultimate and absolute rights of Human Nature, cherished and practised by the first settlers of Virginia, and its constant rebuke by the principles and lives of the Puritans, was the origin, and continued to be the cause, of that perpetual hate of the Yankee, which has become the fortieth and most important article of their episcopacy.

Of course many good men, and much virtue, developed at the South—and many evil men, and their vices, marred the aspects of Puritan society—and its renegades, in the persons of peddlers and slavedrivers, have only fanned the flames of Southern hatred of the Yankees.

Throughout Puritania, the culture of the most extreme ideas of the personal, and political, rights of all men, generated that watchfulness and tenacity which engendered the revolutionary contest—while the continual culture of governmentativeness, through the existence of slavery at the South, supplied the lack of other forces for a corresponding opposition to foreign aggression. Here, too, must be excepted that at the North were some slaveocrats, and at the South some liberty-loving men. But the real virtue of the two parties of the country in that great struggle for political freedom, is illustrated by the fact, that Puritanism did four-fifths of the fighting with half as

numerous a population, while the South would not enlist at all
unless the Puritan armies should be commanded by a Southern
general.   Providentially such an one—a Puritan by nature and
life, had already furnished prestige of the requisite greatness—
and in the natural self-abnegating spirit of the Puritan, was
nominated by the most honored voice from New England.
Thus at the first National opportunity, the slaveocracy required
to be propitiated by what did not belong to them—an injustice
they have never failed to repeat at each recurring occasion.
At the conclusion of the War of Independence, the country,
but little acquainted with the radical principles illustrated by
the history of the continual quarrels of the ancient Greek states,
and their final complete subjugation by more consolidated
neighbors—nor by the excessive governmental burdens suffered
by the petty principalities of Germany and modern Italy—
adopted a scheme of confederation consonant with the govern-
mentive jealousy and state pride of slavedom, but which in
time, proved a rope of sand.   The wisdom derived from this
experience led to the development and adoption of the present
National Constitution.

In the formation of this compact, under whose benign influences the citizens have enjoyed a happiness more exalted than
has ever before accrued to any people, the folly of state supremacy was totally ignored, and the Potent Instrument com-
mences, not "We, the States," etc., but, "We, the People of
these United States, do enact," etc.

And this primal statement is illustrated in a practical
degree by the establishment of sixty fundamental propositions,
divided into two hundred and fifty specific items, in which the
States are held subject to the pre-eminent jurisdiction of the
Central Government—and every rood of land, and every human
resident, subjected to its pre-eminent domain.

As a favor of special value to most of our citizens who may
chance to read this essay, the Constitution is here inserted. The
ceaseless efforts of the slaveocracy to eviscerate every vestige of
expression of antislavocratic character, from the literature of the

country have so well succeeded, that but few people are found who have access to that document, which ought most certainly to be in its every paragraph familiar to each voter of the land. And from it the reader will also be able to discover, that notwithstanding the ceaseless claims of the K. G. C.'s, that is, the Cainites of the Gallows Crime, the President, has not yet, during the two years of war. in any essential particular, transcended the powers with which he is invested by this

CONSTITUTION

OF THE

UNITED STATES OF AMERICA.

WE, the People of the United States, in order to form a more perfect union, establish justice, ensure domestic tranquility, provide for the common defence, promote the general welfare, and secure the blessings of liberty to ourselves and our posterity, do ordain and establish this constitution for the United States of America.

ARTICLE I.—*Section 1.*

1. All legislative powers herein granted, shall be vested in a Congress of the United States, which shall consist of a senate, and house of representatives.

Section 2.

1. The house of representatives shall be composed of members chosen every second year, by the people of the several states ; and the electors in each state shall have the qualifications requisite for electors of the most numerous branch of the state legislature.

2. No person shall be a representative who shall not have attained to the age of twenty-five years, and been seven years a citizen of the United States, and who shall not, when elected, be an inhabitant of that state in which he shall be chosen.

3. Representatives, and direct taxes, shall be apportioned among the several states which may be included within this Union, according to their respective numbers, which shall be determined by adding to the whole number of free persons, including those bound to service for a term of years, and excluding Indians not taxed, three-fifths of all other persons. The actual enumeration shall be made within three years after

the first meeting of the Congress of the United States, and within every subsequent term of ten years, in such manner as they shall by law direct. The number of representatives shall not exceed one for every thirty thousand, but each state shall have at least one representative; and until such enumeration shall be made, the state of New Hampshire shall be entitled to choose three; Massachusetts, eight; Rhode Island and Providence Plantations, one; Connecticut, five; New York, six; New-Jersey, four; Pennsylvania, eight; Delaware, one; Maryland, six; Virginia, ten; North Carolina, five; South Carolina, five; and Georgia, three.

4. When vacancies happen in the representation from any state, the executive authority thereof shall issue writs of election to fill such vacancies.

5. The house of representatives shall choose their speaker, and other officers, and shall have the sole power of impeachment.

Section 3.

1. The senate of the United States shall be composed of two senators from each state, chosen by the legislature thereof, for six years; and each senator shall have one vote.

2 Immediately after they shall be assembled in consequence of the first election, they shall be divided as equally as may be into three classes. The seats of the senators of the first class shall be vacated at the expiration of the second year, of the second class at the expiration of the fourth year, and of the third class at the expiration of the sixth year, so that one-third may be chosen every second year; and if vacancies happen, by resignation or otherwise, during the recess of the legislature of any state, the executive thereof may make temporary appointments until the next meeting of the legislature, which shall then fill such vacancies.

3. No person shall be a senator who shall not have attained the age of thirty years, and been nine years a citizen of the United States, and who shall not, when elected, be an inhabitant of that state for which he shall be chosen.

4. The vice-president of the United States shall be president of the Senate, but he shall have no vote unless they be equally divided.

5. The senate shall choose their other officers, and also a president *pro tempore* in the absence of the vice-president, or when he shall exercise the office of president of the United States.

6. The senate shall have the sole power to try all impeachments. When sitting for that purpose they shall be on oath or affirmation. When the president of the United States is tried, the chief justice shall preside; and no person shall be convicted without the concurrence of two-thirds of the members present.

7. Judgment in cases of impeachment shall not extend further than the

removal from office, and disqualification to hold and enjoy any office of honor, trust or profit under the United States; but the party convicted shall nevertheless be liable and subject to indictment, trial, judgment and punishment, according to law.

Section 4.

1. The times, places, and manner of holding elections for senators and representatives, shall be prescribed in each state by the legislature thereof; but the congress may at any time, by law, make or alter such regulations, except as to the places of choosing senators.

2. The congress shall assemble at least once in every year; and such meeting shall be on the first Monday in December, unless they shall by law appoint a different day.

Section 5.

1. Each house shall be the judge of the elections, returns and qualifications of its own members, and a majority of each shall constitute a quorum to do business; but a smaller number may adjourn from day to day, and may be authorized to compel the attendance of absent members in such manner and under such penalties as each house may provide.

2. Each house may determine the rule of its proceedings, punish its members for disorderly behavior, and with the concurrence of two-thirds, expel a member.

3. Each house shall keep a journal of its proceedings, and from time to time publish the same, excepting such parts as may in their judgment require secrecy; and the yeas and nays of the members of either house on any question, shall, at the desire of one-fifth of those present, be entered on the journal.

4. Neither house, during the session of congress, shall, without the consent of the other, adjourn for more than three days, nor to any other place than that in which the two houses shall be sitting.

Section 6.

1. The senators and representatives shall receive a compensation for their services, to be ascertained by law, and paid out of the treasury of the United States. They shall, in all cases, except treason, felony, and breach of the peace, be privileged from arrest during their attendance at the session of their respective houses, and in going to and returning from the same; and for any speech or debate in either house, they shall not be questioned in any other place.

2. No senator or representative shall, during the time for which he was elected, be appointed to any civil office under the authority of the United States, which shall have been created, or the emoluments whereof shall

have been increased, during such time; and no person holding any office under the United States shall be a member of either house during his continuance in office.

Section 7.

1. All bills for raising revenue shall originate in the house of representatives; but the senate may propose or concur with amendments, as on other bills.

2. Every bill which shall have passed the house of representatives and the senate, shall, before it becomes a law, be presented to the president of the United States; if he approve, he shall sign it; but if not, he shall return it with his objections, to that house in which it shall have originated; who shall enter the objections at large on their journal, and proceed to reconsider it. If, after such reconsideration, two-thirds of that house shall agree to pass the bill, it shall be sent, together with the objections, to the other house, by which it shall likewise be reconsidered; and if approved by two-thirds of that house, it shall become a law. But in all cases, the votes of both houses shall be determined by yeas and nays, and the names of the persons voting for and against the bill shall be entered on the journal of each house respectively. If any bill shall not be returned by the president within ten days (Sundays excepted) after it shall have been presented to him, the same shall be a law in like manner as if he had signed it, unless the congress by their adjournment prevent its return, in which case it shall not be a law.

3. Every order, resolution or vote, to which the concurrence of the senate and house of representatives may be necessary, (except on a question of adjournment,) shall be presented to the president of the United States; and before the same shall take effect, shall be approved by him; or being disapproved by him, shall be repassed by two-thirds of the Senate and house of representatives, according to the rules and limitations prescribed in the case of a bill.

Section 8.

The congress shall have power—

1. To lay and collect taxes, duties, imposts, and excises; to pay the debts, and provide for the common defence and general welfare of the United States; but all duties, imposts, and excises shall be uniform throughout the United States:

2. To borrow money on the credit of the United States:

3. To regulate commerce with foreign nations, and among the several states, and with the Indian tribes:

4. To establish an uniform rule of naturalization, and uniform laws on the subject of bankruptcies throughout the United States:

5. To coin money, regulate the value thereof, and of foreign coin, and fix the standard of weights and measures :

6. To provide for the punishment of counterfeiting the securities and current coin of the United States :

7. To establish post-offices and post-roads :

8. To promote the progress of science and useful arts, by securing for limited times, to authors and inventors, the exclusive right to their respective writings and discoveries :

9. To constitute tribunals inferior to the supreme court; to define and punish piracies and felonies committed on the high seas, and offences against the law of nations :

10. To declare war, grant letters of marque and reprisal, and make rules concerning captures on land and water :

11. To raise and support armies ; but no appropriation of money to that use shall be for a longer term than two years :

12. To provide and maintain a navy :

13. To make rules for the government and regulation of the land and naval forces :

14. To provide for calling forth the militia to execute the laws of the union, suppress insurrections, and repel invasions :

15. To provide for organizing, arming and disciplining the militia, and for governing such part of them as may be employed in the service of the United States ; reserving to the states respectively the appointment of the officers and the authority of training the militia according to the discipline prescribed by congress :

16. To exercise exclusive legislation in all cases whatsoever, over such district (not exceeding ten miles square) as may, by cession of particular states, and the acceptance of congress, become the seat of government of the United States ; and to exercise like authority over all places purchased, by the consent of the legislature of the state in which the same shall be, for the erection of forts, magazines, arsenals, dock-yards, and other needful buildings :—and

17. To make all laws which shall be necessary and proper for carrying into execution the foregoing powers, and all other powers vested by this constitution in the government of the United States, or in any department or officer thereof.

Section 9.

1. The migration or importation of such persons as any of the states now existing shall think proper to admit, shall not be prohibited by the Congress prior to the year one thousand eight hundred and eight ; but a tax or duty may be imposed on such importation not exceeding ten dollars for each person.

2. The privilege of the writ of *habeas corpus* shall not be suspended, unless when, in cases of rebellion or invasion, the public safety may require it.

3. No bill of attainder, or *ex post facto* law, shall be passed.

4. No capitation or other direct tax shall be laid, unless in proportion to the census or enumeration herein before directed to be taken.

5. No tax or duty shall be laid on articles exported from any state. No preference shall be given by any regulation of commerce or revenue to the ports of one state over those of another ; nor shall vessels bound to or from one state, be obliged to enter, clear or pay duties in another.

6. No money shall be drawn from the treasury, but in consequence of appropriations made by law ; and a regular statement and account of the receipts and expenditures of all public money shall be published from time to time.

7. No title of nobility shall be granted by the United States ; and no person holding any office of profit or trust under them, shall, without the consent of the congress, accept of any present, emolument, office, or title of any kind whatever, from any king, prince, or foreign state.

Section 10.

1. No state shall enter into any treaty, alliance, or confederation ; grant letters of marque and reprisal ; coin money ; emit bills of credit; make anything but gold and silver coin a tender in payment of debts ; pass any bill of attainder, *ex post facto* law, or law impairing the obligation of contracts ; or grant any title of nobility.

2. No state shall without the consent of the congress, lay any imposts or duties on imports or exports, except what may be absolutely necessary for executing its inspection laws ; and the net produce of all duties and imposts laid by any state on imports or exports, shall be for the use of the Treasury of the United States, and all such laws shall be subject to the revision and control of the congress. No state shall, without the consent of congress, lay any duty of tonnage, keep troops or ships of war in time of peace, enter into any agreement or compact with another state, or with a foreign power, or engage in war, unless actually invaded, or in such imminent danger as will not admit of delay.

ARTICLE II.—*Section* 1.

I. The executive power shall be vested in a president of the United States of America. He shall hold his office during the term of four years ; and, together with the vice-president, chosen for the same term, be elected as follows :

2. Each state shall appoint, in such manner as the legislature thereof may direct, a number of electors equal to the whole number of senators

and representatives to which the state may be entitled in the congress ; but no senator or representative, or person holding an office of trust or profit under the United States, shall be appointed an elector.

3. The electors shall meet in their respective states, and vote by ballot for two persons, of whom one at least shall not be an inhabitant of the same state with themselves. And they shall make a list of all the persons voted for, and of the number of votes for each ; which list they shall sign and certify, and transmit sealed to the seat of the government of the United States, directed to the president of the senate. The president of the senate shall, in the presence of the senate and house of representatives, open all the certificates, and the votes shall then be counted. The person having the greatest number of votes shall be the president, if such number be a majority of the whole number of electors appointed ; and if there be more than one who have such majority, and have an equal number of votes, then the house of representatives shall immediately choose, by ballot, one of them for president ; and if no person have a majority, then, from the five highest on the list ; the said house shall, in like manner, choose the president. But in choosing the president, the votes shall be taken by states, the representation from each state having one vote ; a quorum for this purpose shall consist of a member or members from two-thirds of the states, and a majority of all the states shall be necessary to a choice. In every case, after the choice of the president, the person having the greatest number of votes of the electors shall be the vice-president. But if there should remain two or more who have equal votes, the senate shall choose from them, by ballot, the vice-president.

4. The congress may determine the time of choosing the electors, and the day on which they shall give their votes, which day shall be the same throughout the United States.

5. No person, except a natural born citizen, or a citizen of the United States at the time of the adoption of this constitution, shall be eligible to the office of president ; neither shall any person be eligible to that office who shall not have attained to the age of thirty-five years, and been fourteen years a resident within the United States.

6. In case of the removal of the president from office, or of his death, resignation, or inability to discharge the powers and duties of the said office, the same shall devolve on the vice-president ; and the congress may, by law, provide for the case of removal, death, resignation or inability, both of the president and vice-president, declaring what officer shall then act as president ; and such officer shall act accordingly, until the disability be removed, or a president shall be elected.

7. The president shall, at stated times, receive for his services a compensation, which shall neither be increased or diminished during the period

for which he shall have been elected; and he shall not receive within that period any other emolument from the United States, or any of them.

8. Before he enter on the execution of his office, he shall take the following oath or affirmation:

"I do solemnly swear (or affirm) that I will faithfully execute the office of President of the United States; and will, to the best of my ability, preserve, protect and defend the Constitution of the United States."

Section 2.

1. The president shall be commander-in-chief of the army and navy of the United States, and of the militia of the several states, when called into the actual service of the United States. He may require the opinion, in writing, of the principal officer in each of the executive departments, upon any subject relating to the duties of their respective offices; and he shall have power to grant reprieves and pardons for offences against the United States, except in cases of impeachment.

2. He shall have power, by and with the advice and consent of the senate, to make treaties, provided two-thirds of the senators present concur; and he shall nominate, and by and with the advice and consent of the senate, shall appoint ambassadors, other public ministers and consuls, judges of the supreme court, and all other officers of the United States whose appointments are not herein otherwise provided for, and which shall be established by law. But the congress may, by law, vest the appointment of such inferior officers as they think proper, in the president alone, in the courts of law, or in the heads of departments.

3. The president shall have power to fill up all vacancies that may happen during the recess of the senate, by granting commissions, which shall expire at the end of their next session.

Section 3.

1. He shall from time to time, give to the congress information of the state of the Union, and recommend to their consideration such measures as he shall judge necessary and expedient. He may, on extraordinary occasions, convene both houses, or either of them; and in case of disagreement between them, with respect to the time of adjournment, he may adjourn them to such time as he shall think proper. He shall receive ambassadors and other public ministers. He shall take care that the laws be faithfully executed; and shall commission all the officers of the United States.

Section 4.

1. The president, vice-president, and all civil officers of the United States, shall be removed from office on impeachment for, and conviction of treason, bribery, or other high crimes or misdemeanors.

ARTICLE III.—*Section* 1.

1. The judicial power of the United States shall be vested in one supreme court, and in such inferior courts as the congress may, from time to time, ordain and establish. The judges, both of the supreme and inferior courts, shall hold their offices during good behavior; and shall, at stated times, receive for their services a compensation, which shall not be diminished during their continuance in office.

Section 2.

1. The judicial power shall extend to all cases in law and equity arising under this constitution, the laws of the United States, and treaties made or which shall be made, under their authority; to all cases affecting ambassadors, other public ministers and consuls; to all cases of admiralty and maritime jurisdiction; to controversies to which the United States shall be a party; to controversies between two or more states; between a state and citizens of another state, between citizens of different states, between citizens of the same state claiming lands under grants of different states, and between a state, or the citizens thereof, and foreign states, citizens or subjects.

2. In all cases affecting ambassadors, other public ministers and consuls, and those in which a state shall be party, the supreme court shall have original jurisdiction. In all the other cases before mentioned, the supreme court shall have appellate jurisdiction, both as to law and fact, with such exceptions, and under such regulations as the congress shall make.

3. The trial of all crimes, except in cases of impeachment, shall be by jury, and such trial shall be held in the state where the said crimes shall have been committed; but when not committed within any state, the trial shall be at such place or places as the congress may by law have directed.

Section 3.

1. Treason against the United States shall consist only in levying war against them or in adhering to their enemies, giving them aid and comfort. No person shall be convicted of treason, unless on the testimony of two witnesses to the same overt act, or on confession in open court.

2. The congress shall have power to declare the punishment of treason; but no attainder of treason shall work corruption of blood, or forfeiture, except during the life of the person attainted.

ARTICLE IV.—*Section* 1.

1. Full faith and credit shall be given in each state to the public acts, records, and judicial proceedings of every other state; and the congress may, by general laws, prescribe the manner in which such acts, records, and proceedings, shall be proved, and the effect thereof.

Section 2.

1. The citizens of each state shall be entitled to all the privileges and immunities of citizens in the several states.

2. A person charged in any state with treason, felony, or other crime, who shall flee from justice, and be found in another state, shall, on demand of the executive authority of the state from which he fled, be delivered up, to be removed to the state having jurisdiction of the crime.

3. No person held to service or labor in one state under the laws thereof, escaping into another, shall in consequence of any law or regulation therein, be discharged from such service or labor; but shall be delivered up on claim of the party to whom such service or labor may be due.

Section 3.

1. New states may be admitted by the congress into this Union; but no new state shall be formed or erected within the jurisdiction of any other state, nor any state be formed by the junction of two or more states or parts of states, without the consent of the legislatures of the states concerned, as well as of the congress.

2. The congress shall have power to dispose of, and make all needful rules and regulations respecting the territory or other property belonging to the United States; and nothing in this constitution shall be so construed as to prejudice any claims of the United States, or of any particular state.

Section 4.

1. The United States shall gurantee to every state in this Union a republican form of government, and shall protect each of them against invasion; and, on application of the legislature, or of the executive, (when the legislature can not be convened,) against domestic violence.

ARTICLE V.

1. The congress whenever two-thirds of both houses shall deem it necessary, shall propose amendments to this constitution; or, on application of the legislatures of two-thirds of the several states, shall call a convention for proposing amendments, which, in either case, shall be valid to all intents and purposes, as part of this constitution, when ratified by the legislatures of three-fourths of the several states, or by conventions in three-fourths thereof, as the one or the other mode of ratification may be proposed by the congress; provided that no amendment which may be made prior to the year one thousand eight hundred and eight, shall in any manner affect the first and fourth clauses in the ninth section of the first article; and that no state, without its consent, shall be deprived of its equal suffrage in the senate.

ARTICLE VI.

1. All debts contracted and engagements entered into, before the adoption of this constitution, shall be valid against the United States under this constitution as under the confederation.

2. This constitution, and the laws of the United States, which shall be made in pursuance thereof, and all treaties made, or which shall be made, under the authority of the United States, shall be the supreme law of the land ; and the judges in every state shall be bound thereby, anything in the constitution or laws of any state to the contrary notwithstanding.

3. The senators and representatives before mentioned, and the members of the several state legislatures, and all executive and judicial officers, both of the United States and the several states, shall be bound by oath or affirmation to support this constitution ; but no religious test shall ever be required as a qualification to any office or public trust under the United States.

ARTICLE VII.

1. The ratification of the convention of nine states shall be sufficient for the establishment of this constitution between the states so ratifying the same.

Done in convention by the unanimous consent of the states present, the seventeenth day of September, in the year of our Lord one thousand seven hundred and eighty-seven, and of the Independence of the United States of America, the twelfth. In witness whereof we have hereunto subscribed our names.

GEORGE WASHINGTON,
President and Deputy from Virginia.

AMENDMENTS TO THE CONSTITUTION OF THE UNITED STATES.

ARTICLE I.

Congress shall make no law respecting an establishment of religion, or prohibiting the free exercise thereof : or abridging the freedom of speech or of the press ; or the right of the people peaceably to assemble, and to petition the government for a redress of grievances.

ARTICLE II.

A well regulated militia being necessary to the security of a free state, the right of the people to keep and bear arms shall not be infringed.

ARTICLE III.

No soldier shall, in time of peace, be quartered in any house, without the consent of the owner, nor in time of war, but in a manner to be prescribed by law.

ARTICLE IV.

The right of the people to be secure in their persons, houses, papers and effects, against unreasonable searches and seizures, shall not be violated; and no warrants shall issue but upon probable cause, supported by oath or affirmation, and particularly describing the place to be searched, and the persons or things to be seized.

ARTICLE V.

No person shall be held to answer for a capital or otherwise infamous crime, unless on a presentment or indictment of a grand jury, except in cases arising in the land or naval forces, or in the militia, when in actual service in time of war or public danger; nor shall any person be subject for the same offence to be twice put in jeopardy of life or limb; nor shall be compelled, in any criminal case, to be a witness against himself, nor be deprived of life, liberty or property, without due process of law; nor shall private property be taken for public use, without just compensation.

ARTICLE VI.

In all criminal prosecutions, the accused shall enjoy the right to a speedy and public trial, by an impartial jury of the state and district wherein the crime shall have been committed, which district shall have been previously ascertained by law; and to be informed of the nature and cause of the accusation; to be confronted with the witnesses against him; to have compulsory process for obtaining witnesses in his favor, and to have the assistance of counsel for his defence.

ARTICLE VII.

In suits at common law, where the value in controversy shall exceed twenty dollars, the right of trial by jury shall be preserved; and no fact tried by a jury shall be otherwise re-examined in any court of the United States, than according to the rules of the common law.

ARTICLE VIII.

Excessive bail shall not be required, nor excessive fines imposed, nor cruel and unusual punishments inflicted.

ARTICLE IX.

The enumeration in the constitution of certain rights, shall not be construed to deny or disparage others retained by the people.

ARTICLE X.

The powers not delegated to the United States by the constitution, nor prohibited by it to the states, are reserved to the states respectively, or to the people.

ARTICLE XI.

The judicial power of the United States shall not be construed to extend to any suit in law or equity, commenced or prosecuted against one of the United States by citizens of another state, or by citizens or subjects of any foreign state.

ARTICLE XII.

1. The electors shall meet in their respective states, and vote by ballot for president and vice-president, one of whom, at least, shall not be an inhabitant of the same state with themselves. They shall name in their ballots the person voted for as president, and in distinct ballots, the person voted for as vice-president; and they shall make distinct lists of all persons voted for as president, and of all persons voted for as vice-president, and of the number of votes for each; which lists they shall sign and certify, and transmit sealed to the seat of the government of the United States, directed to the president of the senate. The president of the senate shall, in the presence of the senate and house of representatives, open all the certificates, and the votes shall then be counted. The person having the greatest number of votes for president, shall be the president, if such number be a majority of the whole number of electors appointed; and if no person have such majority, then from the persons having the highest numbers, not exceeding three, on the list of those voted for as president, the house of representatives shall choose immediately, by ballot, the president. But, in choosing the president, the votes shall be taken by states, the representation from each state having one vote; a quorum for this purpose shall consist of a member or members from two-thirds of the states, and a majority of all the states shall be necessary to a choice. And if the house of representatives shall not choose a president whenever the right of choice shall devolve upon them, before the fourth day of March next following, then the vice-president shall act as president, as in the case of the death or other constitutional disability of the president.

2. The person having the greatest number of votes as vice-president shall be the vice-president, if such number be a majority of the whole number of electors appointed, and if no person have a majority, then from the two highest numbers on the list, the senate shall choose the vice-president. A quorum for the purpose shall consist of two-thirds of the whole number of senators, and a majority of the whole number shall be necessary to a choice.

3. But no person constitutionally ineligible to the office of president, shall be eligible to that of vice-president of the United States.

The fundamental principles of this compact are set forth in
what has been usually termed the Preamble to the Constitution, a very misleading expression, and which should be substi-
suted by something indicating that it is the basis of the entire
document, that it contains not only the corner stones and the
foundation walls which are placed upon the crystal terra firma
of changeless justice. but also the very columns upon which
are supported its magnificent dome. Throughout the entire
extent of the ægis of this constitution. every proposition which
finds expression in that enumeration of principles, is designed
to be absolutely binding in its broadest application, while in the
succeeding sections, each specification of a case of wrong. found
too strongly entrenched in the interests of any faction of parties
to this compact, must of necessity, like Shylock to his pound of
flesh, be limited to the precise, literal, requirements of such
words as describe those exceptions.

And here will the reader permit us to add this suggestion.
that for discerning the meaning of the Constitution, he consult
that instrument itself instead of seeking authorities. which may
mislead. And then, be sure to be governed by Common Sense.
and the Fundamental Basis, that is, the Preamble. Never for-
getting that all questions of doubt are to be determined by the
expression of principles there stated. To illustrate. at this
writing the Cainites whose marked sympathies for all traitors is
a striking feature of the times. howl at every arrest of a sus-
pected wretch, and charge the President with arbitrary disregard
of the safe-guards of the Constitution. Having no sympathy
for it themselves, they ignore the fact that war, and rebellion,
with treason universal. provide the necessities, and the occasions, for which he is armed by the Constitution, and by it
required to act with promptness, decision. and energy.

Reference has already been made to that improvement of the
views of the people which led them to ignore the folly of
attempting to perpetuate the individual nationality of petty
states, and which led them to transfer their patriotism from the
separate states to that of a grander but common empire, and

abnegate their pride of state in behalf of the brilliant glory of a magnificent nationality—thus ascending from the citizenship of a little state to that of an immense and powerful common-wealth—while retiring the states to the position of simple legis-lative and judicial municipalities, only retaining the represen-ative reality of their original independent statehood, in their equal individual representation in the senate of the central government, while relieving that government of the details of local business through their continuance of their original forms of legislative and judicial proceedings, albeit these were now forever limited by the stable requirements of the two hundred and fifty specifications of the National Constitution.

But Jefferson, with the aristocracy of Virginia, could not brook the idea that the Old Dominion, much the largest and most populous of the states, should thus lose that pre-eminence so gratifying to the pride of the slaveocratic character, imme-diately attacked the constitution, endeavoring to persuade the states to pass resolutions limiting the scope of the constitution in regard to this so complete obliteration of state nationality. But with all of his popularity, and his prestige as one of the authors of the Declaration of Independence, he succeeded only in persuading the legislatures of Virginia and Kentucky to endorse his scheme. Ah! could Jefferson have comprehended that he was giving birth to a monster which, feeding upon the envenomed offal of slavery, should, during the lives of men born amid the roar of the revolutionary battles, attempt to extinguish those immortal principles his own hand had incorporated into the fundamental being of the nation, and thus strike the knell of Human Rights, he would have called on God to palsy that hand before it should have made the fatal record, even that God in view of whose justice he trembled when he considered the conflict slavery endangered. Thus were fanned into vigorous life the expiring embers of state rights pride, and from that life has culminated the fearful conflict which threatens the continued existence of this Promise of the Nations.

In seeking for the origin of the political rights of a commu-

3

nity of people to a voice in their political government, the
Fathers of the Republic had been led up to the consideration of
the highest human necessities, and discovered that political
rights accrued from personal rights ; that those, developing
from the nature of things, were inalienable, and that, of this
class, were the right to " life, liberty and the pursuit of happiness." This element of personal rights, incorporated into the
Constitution of the State of Massachusetts, had soon resulted
in the abolition of the little of slavery the British rule had
permitted to develop within her borders, and the remainder
of the Puritanic States, one by one, followed the virtuous
example. But beyond the Puritanic influence, the Slaveocratic
power was too strong for the principles of justice, and the proposition that might makes right, still continued to govern the
development of Southern society.

And the Slaveocracy, with that shrewdness which ever char-
acterizes the cunning of inordinate ambition, in the absence of
moral restraint, apprehensive of the still formidable influence
of the advocates of emancipation, and annoyed by the presence
of the free colored population, developed that splendid delusion,
the African Colonization Scheme, by which at one throw the
sympathy for the enslaved blacks was transferred to the people
of a distant continent, the free negroes removed from close
proximity to the slave, and, most deplorable of all, the way
for a return attack upon slavery, hedged most thoroughly by
the assiduous culture of negro hate.

The Founders of the Constitution, mindful of the fundamental principles involved in the struggle for freedom from political
tyranny, appreciating the origin of those principles in the personal rights of the being, because of his human nature, established those rights as the keystone of the edifice, making the
most important object of the National Compact to consist in
securing the blessings of liberty, to ourselves and our posterity.
Not able to sweep slavery from existence, they were yet so
hopeful of its speedy abrogation, as to use special care, that
while the fact of its existence could not be ignored, necessary

reference to its hateful name, should be in terms that need not recall its sad memory, after it should have ceased to disgrace the Republic.

Their understanding of this element of the Constitution, was early illustrated by the new government, in the immediate passage of the ordinance prohibiting slavery in all the territory then belonging to the nation, and which had been ceded to it by the States claiming the domain of that country between the Ohio, the Lakes and the Mississippi.

In the consideration of this subject, it is all important to appreciate the difference between *what existed in the States prior to the formation of the Federal Government, and what may be created, subject to that Government.*

Thus, while laws in favor of slavery, existing at the time of the adoption of the National Constitution, could not be abrogated by the National Government, because the states having such an institution, were accepted as members of the Union without being required to demolish the same—no laws producing, or legalizing slavery in any state in the Union, could become constitutional, because interdicted by the basilar principles of that instrument, and have not been provided for by any specification releasing such a proposition from the force of that interdiction. The same is true of a territory of the United States—and of the rebellious states whose former laws have been taken without the range of former comity.

As the slaves became numerous in the Southern States, the natural effects of its curse began to exert their baneful influences, producing moral and social blight upon each community where its presence came. The slave plantations being large, and occupying the best portions of the soil, the non-slaveholding population were so much separated as to preclude the possible existence of the District School System, which has been to the North the greatest of her blessings; so that class of the population remained ignorant, and tended to a degradation which challenged the contempt of the slaveholders and the scorn of the slaves.

The planters mostly educated their white children at the North, or employed Northern teachers at home, but the principle associations of their families were with their slaves, who were educated to only lie, and pilfer, and accomplish the least possible amount by their forced labor. Thus, all that makes society at the North delightful, and home a little paradise, is absent from the slave country, occasioning the absence from the South of a large portion of its families, who for blessings not possible there, migrated north of the Ohio. And foreign emigrants, detesting slavery, have flocked to the Free States, so that the South, which in the time of the Revolution, possessed twice the population of the North, has come to exhibit but two-fifths their present number. And in those qualities which go to make up the elements of true nobility of character, the difference in favor of the North is beyond all computation.

Approximate estimates of the pecuniary detriment occasioned to the country by slavery during the last few years, may be rendered sufficiently correct to exhibit its disastrous pecuniary retributions. At the North, out of every family of five persons, at least three of them are laborers at some kind of productive avocation, and earn between them two dollars per day, during three hundred days each year. Now, labor at the South is as productive as at the North, so that of the four millions of slaves, and say six millions of poor whites, whom slavery renders indolent and inefficient—ten millions in all—leaving out two millions as offset by a like number at the North, the ten millions ought to produce four millions per day, which would be for the year, of three hundred days, twelve hundred millions.

The united testimony of all parties acquainted with slave labor, assures that they do not accomplish half as much as free laborers. And the poor whites and slaveholders do as near to nothing as possible. But allow that poor whites and slaves produce half as much as the same number of Northern people —a most liberal allowance—and from this item we discover an annual loss of six hundred millions each year, as the direct effect of the existence of slavery.

Then these two millions of families of slaves and poor whites, living in hovels and shanties, without gardens, orchards, shops and barns, which at the North are worth to each family not less than two hundred dollars per year more than those of the slaves and the poor whites of the South are worth to them, brings in this item a loss to the South, of comforts, to the amount of four hundred millions. Thus, these two items, which closer scrutinizing, will increase instead of diminishing, exhibit pecuniary loss of a thousand millions per year, of which slavery robs its victims, and which has been one of the most irritating and efficient causes of the intense hatred the South has cherished against the North. It were easy for them to contrast their country with the superiority of the North in its increase of wealth and power, but they could only imagine that through the tariff on foreign importations, the North must have robbed them of the earnings of their unpaid slaves. This was the immediate plea for the nullification project thirty years since, although that was the result of the old lust of power and State pride of the Slaveocracy.

Illustrated by the facts with which this essay opens, it would seem that the Slaveocracy foiled in their attempts at nullification, through lack of preparation, at once set about the work in earnest, took time to make their arrangements, and determined to accomplish their purpose, to either subvert the Government of the Union, or break it into fragments.

To this end they began to establish that slavery was a divine institution, and consequently ought to become universal and perpetual. And set about driving from their country all their Northern teachers who would not do homage to this Cainite Gilded Calf—prohibited discussion of the subject, except on one side, and systemized the idea of orders of titled nobility, to be established when they should have "Set aside the forms of Republicanism."

The Democratic party, ever being their efficient ally, led them to believe the North, then asleep upon the subject of personal rights, could with the assistance of that party be made an easy prey, and the slaveocracy settled into a firm confidence that they could easily speak their new despotism into full fledged life. The Democratic party, the ally of slavery—that most intense concentration of despotism! Ah, how many members of the Democratic party open their eyes in amazement at the discovery, that their party, which they had ever believed to embody all the political virtue of the country; that this party they had worshipped as the very god of freedom, did really exist as the powerful right hand of the doubly distilled essence of all despotisms! To a casual observer it certainly is one of those astounding truths which ever seem stranger than any fiction. But the aspect of the case is wonderfully different when viewed in relation to the history of the origin of the party, its name, and the principles involved in its development.

The Slaveocracy, that is, Cainites of the Galling Chains, chagrined by the defeat of their darling idea of State Supremacy, and rendered desperate by the failure of the State Rights resolutions in the State Legislatures, set about the task of acquiring supremacy in the Central Government. Republican liberty was the ruling idea at the time—its votaries were cleansing the Government of the stains, and the curse of slavery. Some effective power must be evoked for the protection of the Slaveocracy, or the gods they worshipped, would be torn from their despotic grasp, to return to them no more. Could they but steal the livery of heaven to serve the devil in, they might yet hope to heal their lacerated pride, and save their gods.

There ever have been in human society three great classes of people, and those classes will ever continue. The first consists of such as always consider the good of all members of community, as a part of the elements which determine their actions, such being the honest worshippers of righteousness, represented by the character of Abel, that is, La Belle, the Beautiful, or the Lovely. The second class is of those whose leading aim is self-aggrandizement, at the expense of any other interest which may seem to be in the way of their success— typified in Cain, and ever seeking to destroy the Abel of society, and ever exclaiming, "Am I my brother's keeper?"

The third and largest class constitute and comprise all those who, less intensely virtuous than the first, and less politically ambitious than the second, are usually content with superficial or one-sided views of political affairs, and free to take the side which most directly appeals to their prejudices, their feelings, the most simply and directly, and to the degree of intellectual acumen, they are usually qualified to bestow upon such subjects. With such elements before them, the Cainite State Supremacy clique, estimated that could they by any means appeal to the motive powers of this third class of society, their object might be successfully attained. Their own principles had been proved to be universally obnoxious to the great majority of the American people—the supremacy of the citizen as against administrators of government—was the ruling idea. By starting a political party, which, while it could be directed by the Cainites, should. through its ostensible motives, appeal to the unsophisticated, and hence unsuspecting masses, the problem of subverting a Republican Government by means of its democratic elements, might be rendered a practical fact. Democracy, the government of a small community by the assemblage and voice of all of its citizens, a temporary incongruity, furnished the most popular cognomen, by which the votaries of free government had been known. By adopting this word as the delusive badge of their party, the fraud would be complete, and the lovers of Republican liberty, marshalled against the temple of their political salvation. It did not avail that the Constitution of the United States already embodied all the democratic elements that could by any possibility become useful, and none but these Cainites of the Galling Chains desired it to become less so. One party being called the Democratic Party, created the inference that all who opposed this party were opposed to the democratic principles of the Constitution. and as a matter of course, when led by the popular name of Jefferson, this new ally of despots carried everything before it.

Coming to be understood by the lower strata of society, to

signify opposition to the strictness of Puritanic morals, it appealed to the licentious, the drunken and the lightfingered. It has ever exhibited in its prints a corresponding grossness of style and quality of language, which has been in marked contrast to the political literature of the Opposition. Never permitting to pass unappropriated an opportunity to stab Puritanism, its alacrity in the service of its Cainite leaders has never faltered from doing their most dirty work. Thus, while it were well to purchase Florida of Spain, and Louisiana of France, that slavery might have more room for the extension of its power, it could refuse to capture Canada, when all things conspired to render that event the most natural, and the most proper thing that could be done. And did this through the disgraceful order for Hull to surrender his entire army to an inferior force, and the recall of Harrison, when having defeated the British and Tecumseh, the enemy had no further power to check his victorious legion. Not strong enough to devote the entire Missouri territory to slavery, contrary to the fundamental principles of the Constitution, it at first secured half of it to this Cainite Gourmand Cyclops, and then, when this part had become occupied, it cooly tramples under foot the considerations of the compromise, and says to the Slaveocracy, take possession. The Cyclops, dissatisfied with the guaranties of the Constitution, respecting the return of fugitives from justice, this ally assists them to the most infamous code for which the world ever had occasion to blush—in the specifications of the odious Fugitive Slave Law of '48 — a law which outrages the essential forms of virtue, and disregards the plainest rights of citizenship. And this, under the false plea of the requirements of that Constitution, whose provisions it so signally disregards.

This subject needs a word of exposition. By reference to the constitution, it will be seen that there is a requirement that " the States shall not pass laws prohibiting the rendition of fugitives from service, or labor, but that such parties shall be returned to the persons to whom such service or labor may be due." But it will not be found in the Constitution that this relates to slaves at all — for legally a slave cannot owe anything — nor can his service be due to any one.

It is claimed that it was meant to apply to slaves. Let it be borne in mind that those making this claim, are strict constructionists. They would bind all by the letter of the Constitution. Their own interpretation then cuts off such application.

To adopt a more liberal position, and admit that the passage was meant to apply to slaves held by legal force, will not assist the claim, for the reason given by the slavocracy who, in '48 would not accept of trial by jury, because the Slave States had no laws by which the unnatural condition was legalized; hence, by their own showing the clause does not apply to slaves, since this specification is in another clause limited to claims of debt sanctioned by law.

But if one more subterfuge be tried, and it is asserted that the States have since passed laws legalizing slavery, we have only to reply that all such legislation is absolutely unconstitutional, as being counter to every fundamental principle of that instrument.

If it is still claimed that it ought to be applied to slaves, out of comity to Cyclops, it is sufficient to reply that too long has the nation been cursed by the practice of this great wrong from comity to Cainite wretches who return the compliment by most treacherous schemes for the destruction of the nation, and the enslavement of ourselves.

But Cyclops, not content with the liberal purchase of non-slave territory for the spread of the infernal institution of savageism —the enactment of the most atrocious laws for its safeguard— the obliteration of every thing pertaining to republican freedom from the literature of the country, and the attempt of the northern Cainites, to follow the southern example of the obliteration of freedom of discussion of the character of slavery— that being too hellish to bear exposure; the slavocracy, not content with all this, and much more, have never ceased to war directly upon the industry of the north, because they could not

endure that necessity of things, that a people, free from the
social curse of slavery, and the crushing weight of aristocratic
dominance, must flourish as the paradise of earth, and the wa-
tered of heaven.

Did northern commerce prosper, war must be evoked to
destroy the commerce. Did the people, driven from commerce
and under the protection of the tariff taxes necessitated by the
national debt, engage in manufactures, then the tariff must be
revised, and the factories stand idle. Did the country with a
stable national currency still grow apace, the currency must be
destroyed till all business is crushed as by a desolating tornado ;
and the sapient instrumentality by which the business of the
country has been " changed these ten times," has of course
never failed to be that potent ally of despotism, the Democratic
party. The cost to the country of all this war upon the industry of the north, man cannot number—but one element may
be introduced as an illustration of the whole. It is drawn from
the subject which formed the ostensible complaint of the seces-
sionists, in the attempt of disruption under the name of nullification. Jackson, being a Republican Democrat, instead of a
Cainite, and understanding the thing in its true light, crushed
the scheme in its germ, but could not annihilate its spirit.
He cautioned the country that it would make a renewed
attempt to destroy the Republic; and that its next pretext
would the subject of slavery. The final extinction of the national debt furnished an opportunity—and as usual the people
were plied with sophisms upon the subject of free trade, and
the unrighteousness of tariff taxation, and the protective tariff
was destroyed.

The people being cajoled into acquiescence, mostly by the
false idea that a protective tariff, by increasing the cost of the
raw material, made living more expensive; and that this
increase of cost of material, enabled the foreign competitor,
even under high duties, to undersell, and thus break down our
own manufactures.

Of course, during a change of the industry of the country,

the price of some elements of production will increase to a greater extent than the tariff increases the price of the foreign article. But all such results would cease, so soon as the business of producing should have had time to develop a supply commensurate to the demand. But the real necessity for a protective tariff arises from the credit mode of doing business, which enables the foreigner with his immense capital, and low rate of interest, to give longer time than is possible to the American manufacturer; and thus make sales to the credit purchaser, who pays him a higher price, in consideration of the greater length of time for making his returns. But this comparatively trifling difference of price between the foreigner and the home manufacturer, might be disregarded, and our people continue to exchange the raw material for the foreign manufacture, were it not for this important fact, that *it costs us more than twice as much to pay for labor done abroad, as it does to pay for the same labor done at home.* And then, by this departure from the changeless laws of nature, in the requirement to make the payment, in only a few of the articles the country is adapted to produce; and these the most limited in range of soil, and climate, and the most expensive to develop, at least half the hands, and other sources of production, which should be engaged, and would be performing this labor, were it all done here, are thus compelled to remain idle.

Under this low revenue tariff during the last decade of years, we have been importing at the rate of a million a day, that is, three hundred and sixty millions of dollars per year. Now not less than two hundred millions of this, ought to be produced at home. Because, first, all of the machinery and hands, which would be required to do this work, are thus compelled to remain idle at a cost to the country of just that two hundred millions. To which must be added the transportation of the goods and their pay, the consequent loss of time and other losses, and the profit of the manufacturers—all of which cannot be estimated at less than fifty millions more. An estimate of the difference between the cost of production of such articles as bear transshipment, will also show that while the production of all such articles costs fully the market price for them, most of the other articles of family consumption, such as vegetables, milk, fuel, rent, etc., on which there would be netted more than the above two hundred and fifty millions, is all lost, so that in this item of robbery by slavery, the country has lost five hundred millions a year.

There is one more pecuniary item, good for all times, as against domestic despotism. In the Slave States are not less than five hundred thousand square miles of land, which, had slavery been abolished twenty years since, would have annually increased in value, as indicated by the improvement in the free States, to the amount of one dollar per acre more than it has now done, allowing forty acres of waste land from each square mile, and we have here a loss of six hundred dollars per year, on each square mile; and which on five hundred thousand square miles would amount to the sum of three hundred millions.

And to this we may add, for village, city, and other improvements, not less than two hundred millions per year, making together the sum of five hundred millions a year, of loss from the prevention of the increase in the value of real estate. To which add the five hundred millions of loss occasioned by slavery's destruction of the protective tariff.

The four hundred millions lost to the South in the form of the comforts of home.

And the six hundred millions lost through the indolence generated at the South by the conditions of slavery. Thus we have, by slavery, a grand total loss, in pecuniary value, of the enormous sum annually of two thousand millions of dollars. A sum greater than the annual cost for both parties in this death struggle for the mastery, between Republican Civilization and Slaveocratic Desolation. An annual sum much greater than was ever claimed to be the market value of the entire slave population. Exhibiting subjection to a despotism more expensive, more intolerent, more destructive of every element of happiness than has been any, which ever elsewhere existed.

One more charge against the Cainite conspiracy of oligarchal despots, in which was involved the Democratic party, as it stood prior to the campaign of eighteen hundred and sixty.

Soon after the suppression of the nullification scheme occurred the first overt attack of the slaveocracy under their revised plan. This was commenced by the imprisonment of William Lloyd Garrison in Baltimore for the crime of exposing certain parties engaged in the nefarious slave trade from Africa, an atrocity outlawed by all nations. He raised the cry of alarm, but the mariners of the ship of State, seduced by the Cainite Gairish Circe, had sailed within range of the enchanting melodies of the Syrens of the Cainite Gourmand Cyclops, and the crew, spell-bound, and lulled to a destructive slumber, exhibited unmistakable signs of the death torpor from which nought less than the bolts of heaven's thunder could, by any possibility, arouse them, and instead of the expected aye—aye—sir—from the Puritanic mariners, the watchmen at mast-head turned a deaf ear, and in Boston a mob of "respectable gentlemen" destroyed his printing office, hunted him as a wild beast, and finally led him in triumph through the streets, with a halter about his neck, as an ovation to the Circe by whom they had been enchanted.

Thus was opened the Puritanic war in self-defence against the tyranny of slavery. Political parties were not then divided strictly upon the slave question, but from that time the Cainism from all parties has been seeking its affinities, till, in the campaign of '56, its entire strength was consolidated in the Democratic party. And it then comprised all of the national slaveocratic sympathy of the country, besides at least an equal number of good honest citizens, who are Republicans by nature ; but who, by birth, training, or other incidental causes, had not discovered that the Cainite Democratic party was not their proper political home.

This party, in both its collective capacity and the individual influence of its members, never failed to make use of every opportunity to oppose and outrage those who endeavored

4

enlighten the nation upon the terrible. calamities developing. and perfecting from slavery.

Through the aid thus rendered by the Cainites of the north. the slaveocracy were led to the belief that, instead of being obliged to abolish slavery, as they certainly would have been obliged to do, but for this assistance from the north, they would be enabled to perpetuate the wretched institution at the south. and to ultimately bring the entire nation under its sway.

Hence the perfecting of their ideas of aggrandizement and their plans for the subversion of Democratic Republicanism. with the establishment of political despotism upon the basis of slavery, while each slaveholder should become a titled noble, and all other persons be disfranchised and ultimately enslaved.

That such were their dreams by night, and their contemplations by day, is corroborated by the direct and explicit statements of their leading men, and every element of information that for years has been evolved from the subject.

Meanwhile, the Cainites at the South, who had since the days of Aaron Burr, continued to cherish the visions of a great slave empire, counting upon this apathetic condition of Puritania, and without due preparation, opened the ball in the form of nullification at Charleston, South Carolina. But the strength of their natural allies being at that time deposited in the loins of Old Hickory, one single gleam of his eye of fire, with the characteristic expression, "By the eternal—John C. Calhoun, if there be one drop of blood shed at Charleston, I will hang you." knocked the scheme into pi, in just the time required for the Vice-President to send his orders to Charleston to "stop all proceedings, because Jackson will hang me if a drop of blood be shed." But the time only, and not the project, was abandoned. Profiting by experience, they at once commenced to secretly organize for the final issue. And emboldened by the success of their Northern allies in their attacks upon Garrison, and the few coadjutors who enlisted in his support, their plan was expanded, so as to include the entire nationality.

Thus, after having together struggled through the war of

Political Rights, the Slaveocracy combined for the subversion of all Human Rights, while the few still wakeful Puritans, in self-defense, associated for the overthrow of slavery, as the only salvation of the country, and the world. But with this characteristic difference, that while the latter were perfectly outspoken, the former obscured their entire movements under the shroud of the most rigid of all secret conclaves.

Thus, in A. D. eighteen fifty, they had all things satisfactory to their seeming, and were " only waiting a convenient opportunity for setting aside the forms of Republicanism." The Iron President Taylor had been dis————(?) of, and the succeeding Vice, had apostatized to the Cainite conspirators—the candidate of the faithful, succeeded in the next election—and apparently but one more cycle of the political machine, was required for the complete subversion of all that remained in the legacy of the Puritans.

All this while the Cainites, as a part of their programme, kept up a continual howl about the violation of the compromises and the guaranties of the Constitution, thus imitating the Gairnish Circe, who ever drove away her virtuous neighbor, by charging her with doing what herself designed to accomplish, and applying to her the name of her own licentious character. Meanwhile, it may be interesting to take a passing review of the facts on this point, before entering upon the next scene in the drama.

The compromises of the Constitution, on the subject of Slavery, are. the continuation of the African Slave Trade, till the year eighteen hundred and eight; and the making of five slaves count equal to three free persons, for the representation in Congress, and the vote for Presidental Electors.

It has been alleged that the Constitution protected the Slave States against National legislation for the extinction of slavery. and that guaranty for the return of fugitives from owed service, included slaves; but there is a perfect absence from the Constitution of any language which can be thus applied. But the North, ever generous to a fault in their courtesy towards the South, have acted upon that allegation, and have even gone so far as to repeal the Personal Liberty Laws, found necessary for the protection of our citizens against the infamous fugitive code of '48. And we challenge the entire Cainite Gibbering Crew, to furnish the first case of trespass against the provisions of the Constitution relating to this subject.

But on the other side, the Fugitive Slave Code of seventeen ninety-three, was unconstitutional, in its abrogation of the trial by jury, where life and liberty were at stake, by returning slaves to States which had no legalized slavery, and as we claim, by giving up men to slavery when there was no requirement for such anti-constitutional proceeding in the Constitution.

The legalizing of Slavery in most of the Slave States since the adoption of the Constitution, is unconstitutional.

The legalizing of Slavery in any Territory in which the treaty for the acquisition of such Territory did not require its toleration, is unconstitutional.

The passage of laws by several of the Slave States prohibiting the emancipation of slaves, unless they be transported from the State, or bonds given for their support, is unconstitutional.

The passage of laws, and the establishment of usuages, which have prohibited the free discussion of the subject, is unconstitutional.

The passage of laws, and the establishment of usuages, by which the residence of citizens holding anti-slavery principles, has been interdicted in many of the Slave States, is unconstitutional.

The passage of the Missouri Compromise Act, by which large Territories and States were given up to slavery, was unconstitutional.

The Fugitive Slave Bill of eighteen forty-eight, by denial of jury trial, and by making the citizens of the North tenders to slaveholders' whelps, is unconstitutional.

The abrogation of the Missouri Compromise, by which the

entire territories of the United States were opened to slavery.
is unconstitutional.

The decision of the Court of the United States that colored
persons have no rights a white man is bound to respect, is unconstitutional.

The Cainite greedy clutching mobs all over the North for the
destruction of Abolitionists, with the freedom of speech and
the press, have all been unconstitutional.

The denial to colored citizens of the rights of the elective
franchise. is unconstitutional.

And the closing of schools and the avenues to wealth, honor
and emoluments to the colored citizens, is unconstitutional.

Thus, with the violations of the Constitution all upon the
side of the Cainite Greedy Cyclops, who never entered into a
compact but to break it, and the maintenance of comity all on
the other side, this concentrated essence of despotism expected
an easy prey of the entire North, the first element of which
absorption, was the opening of all the Territories to the irrup-
tion of slavery.

But the obsequies of the fugitive slave code of '48
were too abject for the endurance of such descendants of the
Puritans, as had not yet forgotten the exalted bequest of their
ancestry, and the disturbance produced by their opposition to
the fines and imprisonments imposed by that odious unconstitutional act, startled many of the sleeping Northerners from
their delusive dreams.

The virgin bosom of Kansas reposed beautifully invit-
ing, the cynosure of all eyes, admired by the liberty-loving, but
most ardently coveted by the destroying Medusa. Votes in the
Convention for the organization of the Territorial Government
were to decide the future destiny of the incipient State. The
vigilant of both parties exerted themselves to the utmost to
secure the majority in the Convention—the Northerners by
bonafide settlers. The Southerners, failing in this, according to
their traditional habit, resorted to every possible subterfuge to
intercept or defeat the efforts of that triumphant tide which

was setting into the imperilled land. Every obstacle was interposed to prevent the "Hated Yankees" from traversing the natural route through Missouri—even to the laughable employment of a "Shibboleth," in the form of a magnificent cow, there being a degree of difference in the pronunciation of the word by the citizens of the different sections of the country. St. Joseph, Mo., was the most direct line of travel, and it was twenty-five miles to the next ferry down the river. So the cow was kept at St. Josephs, and every traveller was required to pronounce the name of the animal. If they said Kaow, then it was all right, and he was passed over. But if he spoke it Keow, he was an Abolitionist, and turned back.

Lest this item should be received as a myth, the writer will add that he has it from the family with whom his home has been during the last three years, and who during several weeks boarded with the people who had then possession of that same cow, and knew her history, having obtained her from the persons who had kept her for that purpose. This fact illustrates the littleness to which the Cainites resorted for the accomplishment of their darling project of the extension of slavery.

But of a different character were the raids of Border Ruffians from Missouri, who entered the Territory armed; and pillaged, burned and murdered such as they considered obnoxious. The peaceful citizens appealed to the National Government for protection, and National dragoons were sent to them, but only to disarm the Republicans, who having despaired of succor from the Cainite Administration, had begun to provide for self-protection. And all parts of the South sent in guerrillas at the time of the Territorial election, to both vote unlawfully and to keep Republicans from the polls.

The settlers of Kansas being from all parts of the country, the recital of the wrongs inflicted by the Cainite clan aroused the descendants of the Puritans to an appreciation of the danger looming above the Southwestern horizon, and marshalled them in solid phalanx to the rescue of the beleaguered people of freedom.

Selecting for their standard bearer the intrepid Fremont, whose sagacity and energy had secured to us the Golden Gateway to the Pacific, and then preserved it from slavery's blighting curse ; heavy majorities for the preservation of the behests of the Constitution, perfectly mapped Puritania, that portion of the continent to which the meeting-house, the school-house, the newspaper, and the lyceum, had transmitted the great leading principles of the original Puritans. While in the Free States, those portions which had been settled by such as to escape the mildew of slavery, had migrated North, but yet retained their former prejudices and sympathies; the cities entangled by commercial relations with the South, and the new States and Territories, where government patronage had moulded the politics, all exhibited large majorities for the Cainite Gilded Candidate, while no Republican development was permitted in the Slave States. With the President, Vice-President and both Houses of Congress, it would superficially seem that the Gourmand Cyclops should have been very self-complacent over his victory. But this first campaign of Republicanism arrayed against the monster for self-protection, had shivered his delusive dream of universal empire. Puritania could not be enslaved nor seduced to grace his triumphal march. The avalanche of Northerners upon the Territories could never be countervoted—soon Republicanism would control the National Government, and the Cainite domination would be at an end.

Giving up the Free States, as past hope of subversion, Cyclops must needs make use of that present auspicious moment for securing the South to slavery and political absolutism. It might become impossible to elect another so willing cats-paw as the Old Buck, the symbol of change. Knavish Greedy Cainites were placed at the heads of the Departments; the Government was run into the greatest degree of insolvency ; the arms and munitions of war were deposited in the Slave States, at such points as would be most convenient ; the war vessels were dismantled in the Southern ship-yards, or dispersed in the most distant seas ; and the preparatory heresy of non-coercion of States was most extensively ventilated.

But one thing more remained to be done. It were still impossible to secure the coöperation of the masses of the citizens of the Slave States, unless they could be cajoled into the idea that the North were such trespassers as to require armed resistance to their invasion of the rights of the South in disregard of the Constitution. Their ordinary mode of making lies and swearing to their truth, always sufficient for an ephemeral election campaign, would too soon, by its transparency, expose the hollowness of the trick ; hence there must be some practical fact, capable of being applied like the proverb : " Spoil the flax and lay it to the hens ;" and this too, after the common Cainite pattern. More than this must be done. Without an interference of the most effectual character, Cyclops' candidate for the next Presidential campaign would inevitably be elected, and supported by a majority in the Senate, and such conditions would afford no room for a justifying argument. Nothing short of the election of the Republican candidate, could be depended upon for the basis of a sufficient lie to excuse the contemplated secession of the Slave States. For this purpose the Cainite party must be rent in fragments. Their National Convention at Charleston, South Carolina, held commission to execute this behest of Cyclops. Douglas, who had bowed and scraped, and fawned, and knelt, and bellied, and paddled in the mire, gulped down the Missouri Compromise and Squatter Sovereignty into the Territories. Douglas, the Little Giant of all Democrats, was, with all the faithful of the North, cast overboard with as little ceremony and less compunction than was the ancient Jonah. The scheme is complete ; the game works to perfection. Of course the Northern Democrats nominate Douglas. Of course the Secesh nominate a Knavish Garrulous Cainite of the most intense degree. And then to make certainty doubly sure, lest by some mishap Douglas should succeed, put upon the course an Old Line Whig, to catch all the Silver Grays, who being too Anti-Republican to go for Lincoln, might otherwise vote for the Little Giant. The result was gloriously beautiful. The Republican President is declared elected by every vote from the Free States in the Electoral College, except the Railroad half of the delegation from New Jersey.

To such perfection did this scheme of Cyclops work, that even in California, where the Republicans were scarce, the votes were so divided among the four candidates that the Republican ticket was elected, though receiving less than one-third of the votes polled. Thus, by a great effort, and a rare combination of cunning, Cyclops succeeded in obtaining the election of a Republican President and Vice-President, opening the way for the preparation of the Southern population, a task not difficult for those who had so long practised the principle established by Amos Kendall, when in the Executive Cabinet, "To meet the statements of the Opposition with lies, because, it is easier to publish half a dozen lies, than to counteract one truth;" and still easier South, where the Opposition might not be heard.

Soon as arrangements could be completed, Cyclops' convention to develop a Constitution for the Slave Confederacy met, and according to a prediction written in '52, "Seven States went down together," that is, combined in rebellion against the government of the United States. Slavery was made the corner-stone of the Confederacy, but as the disfranchisement of the non-slaveholding whites was not included, as being too great a stretch for present possibility, one of the leading Cainites of South Carolina wrote to the Convention, strenuously urging the importance of cutting off this Democratic element, because that, as it was their object to establish an oligarchy of slaveholders, and reduce all "poor whites" to the level of serfs, another war for their purpose would be required. This clearly exhibited the character of the movement, but which the more shrewd of the conspirators possessed sufficient sagacity to keep from view, till the services of that same class, so essential for the war of the rebellion, should cease to be necessary.

The bulk of the army had been stationed at the greatest possible distance from the future scenes of their usefulness, and as far as possible, placed under Secesh commanders. The forts in the Slave States were left without sufficient garrisons to care for the property, while the Capitol of the Nation was rendered almost perfectly defenceless. Buchanan and his Cabinet were all Cyclops could desire, until the Congress began to arouse from its fancied security, and obtained the change of some of the Secretaries.

Cainites' not in the profoundest secrets of Cyclops, made several attempts to assassinate the President elect, while en route for the Capitol, and after the inauguration the Lieutenant-General's sympathies were so much in the interest of the rebels to permit him to order the proper military movements. and the President, too free from guile to suspect others, confided too much in the integrity of dangerous sycophants.

"Whom the Gods will destroy, they first make mad," and the charming facility with which every scheme of the Secesh appeared to succeed, deluded the wretches into the notion that they were the real favorites of heaven, with whom the long-promised millennial glories were soon to open.

But to entrap the border States was a difficult task—something of a thrilling and decisive character was needed to stimulate the timid, and intensify the wavering; the little apology of a garrison in Fort Sumpter, now surrounded by rebel batteries, offered a fine quarry for the chivalry of the south; the little command would be starved out in three days. but the opportunity was too good to be lost.

The last link in the programme was forged; the destinies of the slaveocracy were decided by the capture of the fort; their fortunes were now irrevocably blended; the severance was established; the chain of necessity was ready for binding together the fractions of Cyclops' dominions. But the booming roar of that terrific cannonade like the portentous muttering of a coming earthquake, rolled northward beyond the borders of Secessia, and reverberated through the mountains and over the plains of all Puritania. The memory of Major Anderson and his intrepid command became enshrined in the hearts of all defenders of liberty, where history will embalm them forever. The nightmare enchantment was broken by this sudden awakening of the slumbering millions; the aroused fury of the despoiled, annihilates the trammels, and the boundaries of political parties, and the doom of Cyclops is sealed.

But why—O why did not the Providence of our past behests, and our future hopes, rescue the favored people from this dire calamity? The answer is simple, its import instructive.

America had compromised away her birthright for a pet Gorgon, refusing to strangle the monster, even, while in a death struggle for her own existence. The strangest spectacle the world ever yet exhibited, is this of a people for two terrible years, conducting the most sanguine of wars, for self-protection against the most unmitigated system of evil, possible to trespass upon human rights—that institution endeavoring to destroy the Republicanism, the fathers of this people fought seven years to establish, and yet the degenerate, deluded children unwilling the destinies from heaven itself, should annihilate the unnatural incubus. The bereaved hearts this war causes to mourn, will have occasion to remember that had the Tocsin bell of Garrison been properly responded to by the citizens of the non-slaveholding States, this war would have been averted, and slavery been abolished.

Had the ordinary influences of moral remonstrance failed, this writer knows of a scheme of voluntary emancipation, which would have been introducted in '51, with an absolute certainty of success, but the arrangements of the conspirators fostered by the wet nurses of the North, having become perfect, interdicted any possibility of even introducing the subject, and much more, the practical application. And, since the commencement of the war, it is perfectly plain to those qualified to estimate the inherent forces, that had the north been willing to abolish slavery, and permit the colored people to assist in their own disenthrallment, the first six months of the war would have crushed the rebellion.

The remainder of the carnage and cost of the war must be

considered as the cost of the education of the people back into
the principles enunciated in the Declaration of Independence.
and incorporated into the basis of the National Constitution.
Had we been independent of a providential ministration from
the supernal spheres, the rebellion might then have been nip-
ped in the bud, as was the nullification of '32. But the
chronometer of the world's destiny had struck the hour for the
disenthrallment of the oppressed of all races. The last four
years had signalized the enfranchisement of the serfs of Rus-
sia—the rescue of the Italians from the triple despotism which
had for ages cursed them—all over the world the signs of regeneration become more portentous at each succeeding year,
and the dooms-day of American slavery appeared upon the
dial of 1863. The powers of heaven had been able to find,
but one means at command for the accomplishment of this great
task. Puritania failed to heed the call; the slave country was
too extensive, and military appliances had become too complex
and potent to admit of possibility of success by insurrection of
the slaves; the country was too strong for a foreign invasion of
even all Christendom combined; Cyclops had interdicted both
the voluntary emancipation of slaves, and the discussion of the
subject; nothing remained but to propel the rebellion, all ready
sturdy in its growth, to dimensions so gigantic as to require
the destruction of slavery for its defeat.

This accounts for the apparently stupid apathy of the north,
and the idea of the rebels that Providence was on their side.
This design of Providence and the corresponding ministry of
angels controlling human destinies, explains the amazing
problem of a Republican President, and Congress, permitting
traitor Generals to do for the rebels, what all their own forces
could not do, defeat our otherwise invincible armies, and keep
them from speedily crushing the enemy.

This is the only possible solution of the astounding fact that
a President of Republican principles, devoted to the interests of
the country and mankind, during a long year and more, kept at
the head of our magnificent army, a wretch whose only recom-

mendation was the proclamation that "any insurrection of slaves should be put down with an iron hand." A traitor whose first act was to claim a victory where it had been won by Rosecrans, and himself had robbed that victory of its natural fruits; his second, disgraceful treatment of old General Scott; his third, disobedience of the President; his fourth, restraining all the forces from attacking the enemy; his fifth, an attempt to deliver the Capitol into the hands of the enemy by planning to get his army to the opposite side of the rebel forces, with no possibility of being got back; the sixth, sitting down at York-town one hundred thousand strong, before thirteen thousand of the enemy, and waiting for them to reinforce and fortify; his seventh, failing to pursue the routed rebels to Richmond, when nothing but his orders prevented; his eighth, sitting down in the swamps of the Chickahominy to destroy his army by sickness while waiting for the enemy to render the fortifications of Richmond impregnable, and collect a sufficient force to provide the traitor an excuse for getting his army captured; his ninth, setting Casey's Division unsupported half-way from the Chickahominy to Richmond that they might be captured, while all the other Divisions were still back of the Chickahominy; the tenth, retreating a victorious army to the James River, instead of pursuing a vanquished foe into Richmond; his eleventh, going down the river on a vessel, and waiting for his army to be annihilated; his twelfth, disobeying Halleck's orders to make speedy time back to Washington, to co-operate with Pope; his thirteenth, refusing to send supplies to Pope at Bull Run; his fourteenth, plotting with his brother traitors to get an appointment to the command of the army in Maryland; his fifteenth, moving that army at the rate of six miles a day; his sixteenth, accomplishing the loss of Harper' Ferry; his seventeenth, permitting the shattered rebel to escape from Antietam; his eighteenth, refusing to follow the rebels up the Shenandoah; his nineteenth, repeated disobedience to his superiors; his twentieth, his systematic endeavors to corrupt the army of the Potomac.

5

Such is the damning record of the hero of the Cainite party of the North. Such the material of which that party is laboring to make a candidate for the next Presidential campaign.

As the dismissal of Fremont from the command of the Department of the West opened the way for the return of the rebels to the districts from which he had driven them, by which four months of time were directly lost, and the enemy enabled to so fortify the Mississippi that we have not yet been able to open that important thoroughfare.

So Buell's removal of Mitchell from Tennessee, provided for the rebel incursion into Kentucky, and Buell had previously planned to secure the annihilation of Grant's army at Pittsburg Landing, but was foiled by Nelson, who, in disobedience to Buell's orders, crossed the river in time to prevent such a catastrophe.

And the appointment of Pope to the army of Virginia where the appointment belonged to Fremont, who had just driven the enemy from the valley of the Shenandoah, and who then would have occupied Gordonsville, the key to the valley,—provided for all the sickening carnage of the incursion of the rebels into Maryland.

It would seem that this constant reverse of our forces, when the righteous idea of the disenthrallment of the slaves was trampled under foot by the displacement of those officers who pre-eminently represented that idea, would have opened the understanding of the Northern people to the pointings of Providence, as indicating a demand to " Let the oppressed go free." This may have been one of the most effectual considerations inducing the Executive to proclaim the freedom of such as the rebellion had already absolved from all legal servitude. But the Cainite gallows criminals of the North, taking advantage of what oppposition still remained to the abolition of slavery, assisted by all their Cainite gulled calves, which, like calf buffaloes, implicitly follow any hunter who, finding them asleep, shall hold his hands over their eyes till they take his scent ; by the Cainite greasy calves, who are afraid of an expected conscription ; by the Cainite guzzling crew, who esteem a good drunk above all the behests of republican civilization ; by Cainite grasping clutchers, who to get rich, seduce their neighbors to ruin, that themselves may filch their property from them ; and by the Cainite Gomorrah cravens, who combining the dram shop, the gambling den, the bawdy theatrical, and the lewd chamber, in one hellish maelstrom, to prey upon victims, who being once drawn within its yawning vortex, rarely escape. Such were the precious combination of hell's best, who under the panoply and prestige of the perpetual and faithful ally of Cyclops, the Democratic party, by a tremendous effort of lying, and every other possible fraud, and in the absence of the Republican voters, who constitute the bulk of the army, carried the late elections in the middle States. This effort seems to have been a last desperate throw of the Cainites of the gallows crime, both North and South, in concert with the doings of McClellan and Buell, with the spasmodic incursions of the rebels east and west to make one more effort to bring all of the North, except New England, under the slave power, through the restoration of the supremacy of the Democratic party, and yielding up the National Government into the hands of Cyclops in the election of sixty-four, should it be possible to so hinder the military operations as to prolong the war till that time. The Democratic party—it is to be regretted that necessity compels the application to American citizens, of that name, which is doomed to be in history the term which will more than all others combined represent the greatest degree of unrighteous villainy. this party, elated by their success at the elections, cast off the mask, boldly avowed their intentions to subvert the government. and increased their appliances for the ruin of the armies. But the soldiers, indignant beyond expression, gave them such a response as has compelled them to change their tactics to the more dangerous plan of apparent acquiescence in the motions of the Administration while to more secretly sap the foundations of its power.

Having strenuously opposed the employment in the army of colored people, whether free or slave, and secured the cessation of volunteer enlistments, the Democratic members of Congress, in a solid column, voted against a conscription themselves had rendered the only means by which the army could be replenished. They now, taking advantage of the misapplied leniency of the Administration, are taking the stump. talking treason and urging resistance to the draft. And with their usual degree of brass, allege that the draft was ordered for the purpose of persecuting the Democrats,—because, forsooth, four-fifths of the volunteers were from the Republican party, and the other fifth were those who by nature belong to Republicanism. Poor fellows! there is no relief for them, for although resistance to the draft is talked of, nothing would more please the outraged Patriots in the army than to be commissioned to expunge that class of traitors. They dare not involve such demonstration, and the more shrewd of the Cainites have begun to double upon themselves and chew their criminal speeches. Thus stand affairs after two years of terrible war for the life of

Republican Civilization, and of our Nation, its only stable home. A convenient occasion for recounting the results thus far of the contest.

Commencing with hardly the germ of either army or navy, with deeply seated determination on the part of the government, and of nine-tenths of the people, to wage the war so as by all means to preserve Cyclops, with the fifteen slave states either in actual rebellion, or waiting till the proper time to become so, with no power but the national military to prevent, and every department of the government benumbed by the presence of disguised traitors of every degree, from such as desired the universal establishment of despotism, with slavery, to those who only care to enrich themselves by plunder from any possible source, and any sacrifice of carnage to the country.

Naval warfare has been completely revolutionized. A naval power superior to any other afloat, has been created, and all places in the hands of the rebels, to which the navy can approach, excepting Mobile, Savannah, Charleston, Wilmington, Vicksburg, Port Hudson, and Galveston, have been captured from the enemy.

A volunteer army of eight hundred thousand (800,000) men has been enlisted, armed and equipped, and fought more battles and kept up a longer stretch of lines than was ever known in any other war, and have subdued the rebellion from all except an equivalent of five and a half states; divided the Old Dominion, and secured the abolition of slavery in the new State of West Virginia, and opened the ball of Emancipation in Delaware, Maryland, Missouri, Kentucky, and Tennessee, and determined the extinction of slavery in all the remainder of Secessia. A large majority of the people are converted to the necessity, if not to the duty, of the abolishment of slavery in the rebel states, and are becoming convinced of the propriety of enlisting the freed men into the army. This also is manifestly a part of the progress of the Providential destiny which forces this great movement forward, whether human people favor or oppose. Because, that after peace be restored, the condition of the colored people of the cotton states will require that they should become qualified to protect themselves from the rapacity of their Cainite neighbors. And it will not be very strange if the National Government finds a necessity for extending to them the rights of the elective franchise, as the means by which to secure in those states obedience to the requirements of the Constitution.

The despotic elements in the governments of France and Britain, like hungry dogs fearing to get sore heads, keep up a constant snarling—the former, to vent his spleen, pitching into Mexico, with the result of uniting that distracted people in the support of the anti-Jesuit government—and the latter, covertly fitting out blockade-running merchant vessels, and an iron-clad pirate navy, for the benefit of the rebels. All of which will evoke special Jesse, when the day of reckoning comes.

This last idea brings us round again to the Democratic party, which, as if its infamy could not else appear complete, when a war with Britain is imminent—assisted by the interest of Rail-road Corporations, accomplished the defeat of the plan for admitting gunboats through enlarged locks in the Erie, and Illinois canals—thus continuing the defenceless condition of the lakes, whose towns are all exposed, and whose commerce is double the entire foreign trade of the nation. And a scheme, the execution of which will enhance the pecuniary interests of every citizen of the Northern States, from Maine to California. This explains why the President, and General Agent, of the New York Central Railroad have been members in the Thirty-seventh Congress, where their influence could be most fatally exerted to defeat this most important measure—that being a darling project of the railroads.

Let the citizens of Puritania remember, that since the sun of slavery is set, this railroad combination is the most dangerous enemy, likely to attempt the subversion of Republican Liberty— that assisted by the Democratic Party, they have only been hindered from robbing the country of the behests of the great Clinton river, by the sudden uprising of the Republican Party —stimulated by the proprietors of ten millions of property per-taining to the canal commerce, which the State of New York was obligated to protect, and which the fraudulent proceedings of the Central Railroad Company had at one time consigned to useless decay. Let it be fully comprehended that the speedy enlargement of the capacity of these canals, so as to permit the passage through them of vessels, as large as can profitably do business on the lakes, is the only means by which the grasping railroad combinations can be prevented from acquiring control of the elections, and the commerce, and consequently of the liber-ties of the people. In this nefarious scheme they will count upon the assistance of all the allies of the Democratic Party. One of these, the brothel interest, has not been openly known as an element in politics, until the Gubernatorial campaign of '62, when in the form of the concert saloon interest, in which was combined all that can be marshalled to the destruction of morality, and in short, all virtue, it gave the casting vote of thirty thousand in New York City, by which the twenty thousand majority from the Puritans of the rural portion of the state, were rendered nugatory. Their slavocratic ally will soon expire—but their old right-bower, grog, begins to show signs of renewed vigor, and must receive special attention. It is about forty years since the American people began to become alarmed by the extent of the ravages of alcoholic intoxication, and the rapid increase of drunkenness, which threatened to whelm the entire population in one common ruin. Entering into the domestic, and the social habits of the people—it had become one of the controlling institutions of the land. Ubiquitous, it had invaded the nursery, the kitchen, the pantry, the parlor, the shop, the field—in short, wherever people labored, or visited, or recreated, there was the monster found —and thence his conscripts marshalled. His besotted victims numbered three hundred thousand (300,000) strong, when the population of the nation was about twelve millions—and his annual slaughter of human sacrifices being ten per cent. of the sots, amounted to thirty thousand. The descendants of the Puritans rebelled against such vassalage, and through the indomitable energy, and perseverance, for which the race is distinguished, succeeded in rolling back the swelling tide, and have almost completely rescued these departments of life, from the polluting presence of the ruthless destroyer. Perfect success seemed about to crown the victorious Abel of Temperance—when the gorgon found shelter behind the counter of the inn-keeper, where, protected by the ægis of that ever ready ally of any Cainite Grievous Curse. the Democratic Party—it has during many years stood at bay, gnashing, and foaming, at all opponents, and taking many prisoners from the unwary who chanced within his reach. The Temperance Army never proposed the use of other means than persuasion, and moral influence, to prevent men from using the destroying draught. But in the Cainite style of misrepresentation, the political allies of drunkenness, made such charge a specific power, in use against both the moral force brought to bear against the drinking, and the political power arrayed against the privilege of making taverns, and hotels, and groceries where people's business required them to be—specially and legally endorsed—institutions for enticing the else virtuous to deepest ruin. The common Cainite question has been—"What! deny me the privilege of drinking what I please?" That has not been proposed—nor will it be. But Cain—be assured of this, that, other people have rights, and it is the fundamental principle of the Constitution of this nation, that those rights, and the privilege of their exercise, are to be protected—and that principle was transcribed from the eternal laws of existing Nature. Are you a husband—the wife of your bosom has a right to clean breath, the respectability of a sober man's home, and an honored partner's society. Are you a wife—the husband of your choice has a right to the possession of an unsullied jewel. Are you a parent—you have assumed an obligation from which naught but death can absolve you, to provide for the necessities, the culture, and the honored name of the children of your plighted vows. Are you a child—the parents to whom you are indebted for being, care, and manhood, have a right to be honored in your nobility, and in their declining years, sustained by your respondent care. Yes, Cain, it is not only the right, but the imperative duty, of society, to protect its members from the desolating devastations of alcoholic intoxication. You will be left to drink what you choose—so long as the drinking does not invade the rights of others. But from time immemorial, society has exercised the right to regulate, and limit the sale, and drinking, at places of public resort, of alcoholic beverages, because the circumstances connected with such drinking, do not leave people to their choice as determined in their unexcited moments—but through various influences impels them to drink to excess—and generates destructive habits. The former license laws, based upon the supposition that alcoholic beverages were necessary to the traveler, provided that the tavern should be supplied for such purpose, while all possible restrictions were connected with this arrangement through which the neighboring residents, were to be restrained from being enticed by its presence. Investigation of the subject has settled the question with the established fact, that, alcoholic drinks are not necessary to the traveler—and history has co-ordinately shown, that the habit of drinking such intoxicating beverage at public inns, is of necessity a dangerous element in society—a nuisance of such demoralizing power, as to demand the most emphatic determination of the people, for its extinction. If some will use the poison, let them do as invalids do—carry their doses with them.

Such be the allies, whose aggregated forces, constitute the power of the Democratic Party, which will henceforth be known as the embodiment of all principles of evil, and their unscrupulous supporter. Such be the party, whose history must soon be completed—and from which every consideration of virtue, every exalted aspiration of human nature, every cherished hope of spiritual excellence, demand of all honest men, who, either born in the party, or enticed by the sophism of its unappreciated name, that they cease to associate in fellowship with

Cain—and that like Lot from Sodom, they hasten from its borders, that the smiting angel be not longer hindered. Leave to such as are Cainites by nature, the work of concocting schemes for subverting the rights of the people, and the hindrance of civilization. Leave to those to whom it is natural, to mourn over the extinction of slavery, a portion of whose inflictions have been enumerated in the preceding pages—but whose deeper woes we leave to be accounted by the many millions whose experiences enable them to appreciate its horrors, and whose attorneys, as the Providential Ministry, are at present most terribly adjusting the balance sheets of the record. The expensive sacrifice of a holocaust of martyrs upon the altars of Republican Civilization has this relief. that, while it makes desolate the homes whose circles miss the offered victims—the loss clouds not the recollection with dishonor—and the future kindred of the glorious slain, will worship at their shrines. Leave to the natural Cainite, to foster, and protect, the Concert Saloon, whose atmosphere is pollution. whose entrance is the vestibule of hell, whose ruined victim brings dismay to the household, and whose vacant place chills the heart with an unmitigated anguish. But the experience of those whose sufferings attest the intensity of their desolation, present the record of sorrows this Cainite Circe entails.

Leave to the natural Cainite, to sustain the gorgon of drunkenness, in the form of the legalized dram-shop, whose trade is the manufacture of drunkards, to the desolation of more homes, than be produced by any other destroyer. Had this evil been left to continue to increase, only as the increase of population. at the present time, the drunkards' army would have been seven hundred and fifty thousand (750,000) sots, with an equal number of recruits on drill, besides the incipient militia—exhibiting a greater army than the slave war has yet evoked from both parties to the contest—and an annual slaughter of a hundred thousand victims, whose demise brings relief—whose deeds remain unhonored and unsung—but not unwept.

Leave to the natural allies of the " Sum of all villanies" to repeat the Cainite gibberish cant—" D——d Abolitionists," "Woolly Head," "Black Republicans," "Nigger on the Brain," etc., which serves the double purpose of ventilating the Cainite spleen, and keeping the Cainite graceless calves in the trammels of the party, but is a piece of that tactics which ever applies to the opposite party, whatever disease or folly itself is subject to. Yes, nigger on the brain, from those who long since became monomanics with color-phobia. " Black Republicans," from those whose machinations by alliance with the blackness of slavery, have sapped the foundations of all that is democratic in our institutions. "Abolition war," from the party whose prophet Jackson predicted the rebellion, and which could not have culminated but through the assistance of the party, by drowning the voices raised in warning against the black and lurid storm, seen gathering over the Southern horizon, and which has burst with such unparalleled fury over our devoted land, saved only by the Republican rally around the Constitution, the Capital and the Country. Black—aye black! Let such mono-maniacs not forget it were their own impious hands which brought black drapery of mourning into almost every household of this desolated but erst happy land; and that those sable vestments be the ghosts which shall forever haunt their guilty visions.

Cainites all! Your evil brood have come home to roost, and they eat out your homes forever. Retribution is after you, and no hope of yours is left—no chance for escape, except abdication and perpetual seclusion. The spear of Ithuriel is athwart, your way to unmask your lying sorceries; the bayonets of the outraged Volunteers are behind you, forcing you on to destruction. The indignant angel ministry hovers above you, closing effectually your approach to Heaven. The pit of oblivion yawns beneath you, and its denizens already dance antics, joyfully anticipating your speedy arrival, when they will enjoy, chasing you to the darkest recesses of perdition.

The energy of the Republican party saved the nation from the destruction Cyclops had prepared for it, and the acceptance by that party of the destined overthrow of slavery, though reluctantly, and after passing the most fiery ordeals, has obviated the necessity for an entire breaking up of the foundations of the government, and provides for the final merging of our institutions into that complete and universal system, which the entire world is being rapidly prepared to adopt.

That will be the ultimate, for the development of which Abraham was commissioned to found a series of religious institutions, to consist of five great acts or parts—the Patriarchal, the Servitudal, the Theocratic, the Christian, and the Spiritual. The time for the commencement of the third, of which Abraham predicted; and the times of the commencement of the fourth and fifth, of which were distinctly and explicitly represented by Daniel. That last time has arrived, and the transition of the world into its forms of Christian, or more correctly, its Spiritual Republican Civilization, is rapidly progressing. Four thousand years of special angel ministry has been required to develop the human conditions needful for such final establishment of man upon the beautiful estate of his adult life, and permanent exaltation. The Republicans of to-day are called to the great work of this regeneration of the human people, and upon them devolves in consequence, the most tremendous responsibilities. The conditions of this labor demand the most intense earnestness, and the most ceaseless vigilance, for as the Cainite foes of virtuous civilization find the elements of their doom crushing in upon them from all directions, they whet the edge of their malice, and increase the ingenuity of their devices, for the retention of their grasp upon the spoils of domination. Republicans must follow them even to the seemingly little things, and unmask their sophistries and thwart their plans.

Even at this writing, ere yet the sound of their traitorous utterances have ceased to carry dismay to the hearts of the people, and anguish to the bosoms of the volunteers ; apparently caused by the first ominous tap of the drum and gleam of the bayonets, of that eight hundred thousand outraged soldiers, in response to the threatened reaction at the North, they have cunningly faced about, and already prate as though themselves were the very residuaries of all patriotic virtue. Be not deceived by this light-fingered shuffling of the political cards. Remember it is no new game of theirs. Like herdsmen driving their cattle to the shambles, when a panic starts the cattle back so furiously as to defy all efforts to stop them, they run before the herd till the effects of the excitement have passed off, when they skilfully turn them about, and drive the unthinking herd to certain slaughter. Remember the men of this practise, and let none forget the malignant chuckle with which they ever greet any calamity to the army, and the quickness with which they ventilate their treason whenever misfortune to the government furnishes them a gleam of hope for the success of their nefarious schemes for the destruction of our fair Temple of Liberty.

Neither permit the unwary to be ensnared by the desire of getting a disguised Cainite who is as if he were Nott, to harrangue the people upon the science of government, that he may find a covert opportunity to bleat the doctrines of secesh treason, under the prestige of the institution of literary lectures.

Nor yet be induced to give certain Cainite people too much credit for political virtue, because forsooth, possessing genial sympathies, or religious fervor, or mercantile honor, which renders them apparently amiable, urbane citizens, and hospitable neighbors. Lacking the force of that integrity which might sustain them in the trial hour, they ever, like broken reeds, fail, when really needed for succor. Often possessed of com-

prehensive, far-seeing intellects, like the eagle disdaining the
prey nearest their eyrie, they acquire a reputation for probity at
home, while at a distance many a noble quarry attests the rapacity of their talons. Illustrate this principle by the mangement
of the railroads, as a sample that of the New York Central.
Soon as the keen glances of the big men comprehended the idea
of a consolidated monopoly through the great natural highway
of the nation's internal commerce, through which already
flowed the freighted Clinton River, and that in process of enlargement, to correspond with the growth of trade, scenting a grand
opportunity, and suborning the Democratic party, they secure
the stoppage of that improvement which would soon have been
ready to enrich the nation, and at a cost of a large proportion
in damage of what would have been the cost of its completion.
Next they subvert the law of the charter of the roads by annul-
ing the tolls on their freight business. Then they develop a
system of lake transportation, and control freight from the canal, through purchases at the West, and monopolize the carrying business of the lakes. One more item completes the scheme
by which they were to compel the State to sell them the canal,
when their control of this great system of commerce would
have been complete—the people's control of the State Government destroyed—and the monopoly piled up wealth without
limit through a tax upon this commerce, compared with which
a foreign tariff becomes insignificant. That item was the con-
veying of goods and produce between the East and West, at a
cost hardly exceeding what their published reports assure to be
the cost through this State alone. That is, they report the
absolute cost to them of a barrel of flour from Buffalo to New
York City, to be forty-seven cents, and at the same time were
carrying it from Davenport, Iowa, to New York City at fifty
cents a barrel. And then goods from the East were carried on
the same principle, so that, as an instance, a cabinet-manufac-
turer at Buffalo, was obliged to remove to Connecticut, because
it cost so much more to send West from Buffalo, than from the
latter place, he could not compete with eastern establishments,
though their distance of transportation was five hundred miles
greater. But defeated in this scheme, they are still alert, and
their President and General Superintendent have been in Congress for the purpose of defeating that enlargement of the
locks of the canal, rendered necessary by the rebellion they had
assisted to evoke, because that measure by providing for the
passage of steamers as large as can profitably navigate the lakes,
would forever destroy their hope of obtaining control of this
commerce, and of subverting the liberties of the people. Let

the citizens of all Puritania, and especially the volunteers, re-member that this rich railroad corporation, who pay their Pres-ident a salary just equal to that of the President of the United States, refused to convey a few miles gratis, a returning soldier of Michigan, who had lost a leg and an arm, and had a shot through his upper jaw, but set him off at Canandaigua.

It is not uncommon for railroad companies to have two sets of dividends—a small one for the outs, but a large one for the ins. Men who will practise as above are not too honest to do this, and those who choose may believe such be not the practice of the New York Central. Let it be forgotten that now the slave monopoly is annihilated, and the grog-ruin monopoly crippled, the railroad monopoly backed by the consistent Democratic party, which is ever crying against monopolies, is rapidly grow-ing to be the most powerful, and the most dangerous institution left to threaten Republican Freedom.

In conclusion, let Republicans remember that their task is hardly yet begun. There is for such no rest, until all those foes to the rights of human nature, treated of in these pages, are rendered effete. Be sure to affect permanent systematic organizations in every county, city, ward, and town, in the land. Be diligent and earnest for this great cause of spiritual civiliza-tion. Leave alone all natural Cainites, but with your neigh-bors who are only misguided, labor to open their understand-ings to a realization that whatever of good has been in the Democratic party, that good has left its such abode. Show them that the only important issues are now directly between Republican liberty and despotic tyranny. Be not distracted to the non-essential incidents of personal affairs, but cling closely to the records of history, and the principles *men act.* Remem-ber that in this essay you receive the truths of history, though not cumbered with the statistical demonstrations. Make relent-less war upon the lying policy of the Democratic Press, and build up your own power upon pillars of truth.